MY JOB EXPERIENCE

A Testimony of God's Grace and Mercy

CYNTHIA J. RIOLAND

Dedication

This book is dedicated to my parents, the late Robert and Lucy Jackson who raised me in church and taught me how to love others and serve God. You are greatly missed. I hope you are proud of me.

My Job Experience

Acknowledgements

I want to first acknowledge my Lord and Savior Jesus Christ for creating me, seeing purpose in me and being the God of a second chance. To my wonderful husband who has proven to be my greatest support and cheerleader through the years, I love you beyond words. Thank you for believing in me. To my son, who constantly said, "Mom, follow your dreams and walk in your purpose." You saw my struggle. Thank you.

Thank you to my cousin Monique, who is a physician, my two sisters Gladys and Alva, who were all at my bedside and my brother Robert who helped during my recovery process at home. To Rosie, my spiritual daughter who came to the hospital every day for five weeks, your quiet presence was healing.

To Tracey Harding, Gail Haynie, Stacey Edens and Pam Williams, thank you for holding my feet to the fire. You told me for many years to write my book. Even though this is not the initial book, it was your encouragement and emails literally over a decade asking, "Where's the book?" that continued to inspire me. Thanks for pushing me, believing in me and ensuring that I publish a book. I still have your emails from ten years ago encouraging me.

Thank you to my friends for being there during this difficult season. If I didn't know you were my friend before, I know now. You know who you are.

Contents

Foreword

My *Job Experience: A Testimony of God's Grace and Mercy* will make you cry, laugh and connect with the universal complexities of what we call Christianity. As the reader, you will experience the joy, pain, peace and truth of the author's journey.

This literary testimony provides a unique perspective of the modern day Job in the form of Cynthia J. Rioland, a tenacious and driven woman who conquered a feat of physical, emotional and spiritual proportion. She creatively uses her life-threatening illness to translate into everyday life challenges. She has the uncanny ability to interconnect today's realities with one of the bible's most engaging stories—The Servant Job.

I have known Cynthia Rioland over forty years professionally and socially. I have personally witnessed her spiritual growth and maturity. A gifted preacher and highly anointed woman of God, she has inspired from the pulpit and at women's conferences and seminars across the country. Today, she broadens that platform by the releasing of her first published literary work.

She is a woman of impact and passionate about addressing women's issues. She has led women's ministry at numerous churches and has brought growth and change to women of all ages and walks of life through creative means. Her warm inviting spirit is sensed in the pages of this book. Cynthia's transparency and openness is refreshing and life changing.

I invite you to grab a box of tissues, a cup of tea and your favorite snack as you relax and embark upon this easy read.

Rev. Dr. Barbara J. Davis
Professor of Theology
Bethune Cookman University

A Message
to My Readers

My *Job Experience: A Testimony of God's Grace and Mercy* is a book for every sister who has been through something, but did not know its purpose. You will read about a little girl who loves God deeply and serves Him with her whole heart. But she comes upon a season in her life when she finds that her love for God does not exempt her from the challenges of life. She moves from being teased as a little girl for her strong Christian values to a woman wrestling with God over those same values.

This book is a real life testimony of my personal Job experience. I am confident that as you read each page, you will almost think you are reading about your life and forget that it is my story. Perhaps that is the goal, to let you know that you are not alone in what you are going through and although our stories may be different, they really are the same.

As sisters, we don't like to be vulnerable. We like to put a mask on and act as if we have never had those moments when we've asked God, "Why?" Why did I have to go through the loss? Why did I have to go through the abuse? Why did my father leave me? Why did I have to get a divorce? Why do I have to be sick? Why? Why? Why_____, you fill in the blank. In the spirit of true sisterhood, I make myself vulnerable to people who know me, do not know me or think they know me. I ask you to appreciate my transparency because this is not easy at all. The fear of even attempting to write this book was sometimes overwhelming as I pondered if anyone would be interested in what I have to say. If vulnerability were easy, more of us would take off our masks. But I get it. Everybody cannot handle your truth. There's the risk of being judged, criticized, misunderstood or taken advantage of.

Let me forewarn you that this book may evoke a wealth of emotions, but embrace them. See yourself in each chapter or just get in where you fit in, but be honest, so you can come out better. Whatever your Job experience, rejoice in the fact that you are still here, you are a *Testimony of God's Grace and Mercy.*

Introduction

Who is Job? Great question. The correct response is that Job is a biblical character in the Old Testament. He is a righteous man of great wealth who prays for his family every day *in case they have sinned*. However despite his uprightness, with the permission of God—with the caveat that Satan cannot touch his soul—Satan strips him down to nothing through great calamity that happens rapidly and succinctly. First with the loss of livestock, then the death of his ten children through an act of nature, because of the calamity in his life, his friends accuse him of being punished for his sin, and his wife encourages him to curse God and die.

The soul has been defined as the essence or spirit of a person. You can lose a car, a house, your job, a spouse, a child or almost lose your mind. But when you lose your soul, which is the very essence of who you are, you lose your will and desire to live. You lose a sense of who you are. I believe this is why God allowed Satan to touch Job's material wealth through his livestock and his family but not his soul—to show that he was more than the sum total of all his losses.

Maybe that's why you're still here and I'm still here. Not because we haven't lost anything. Not because we haven't experienced disappointment or hurt, but we didn't lose our souls. As women, God has made us resilient and able to recover from whatever obstacles or challenges we may face. Have you had your Job experience yet? No? Well, just keep on living. It is inevitable, so be ready; not by living in fear and trepidation, but with the determination that you will prevail. Ask yourself, "What's the lesson to learn and how will I help the next sister?"

I can tell you that I was not ready for my Job experience, but I prevailed because of *God's Grace and Mercy*. I prevailed because I had a strong foundation built on the word of God and an authentic personal relationship with my creator. I prevailed because in the words of the old song, *Somebody prayed for me, had me on their mind, took a little time and prayed for me!*

CHAPTER ONE

The Early Years

I was born in Washington, D.C. to Robert and Lucy Jackson, the youngest of four children. The bratty little sister who loved to tattletale—that was me. Miss Goody Two-Shoes should have been my middle name. I did not have to wash dishes, do laundry or clean the kitchen because everyone else did it for me. I was the bratty little sister who no one ever wanted to have around, spying on my siblings, eavesdropping on conversations and getting into my siblings' personal items. I was bored and inquisitive, which is a dangerous combination. They took up for me, dressed me and sometimes gave me a spanking (something my parents didn't do.) My father never gave me a spanking because all I had to do was bat my puppy dog eyes, release crocodile tears and he would just scold me. My mother, on the other hand, would politely announce that she was about to smack me and commence to do so with only one powerful swing. That was always sufficient to get me back in line.

People today would call that cruel and unusual punishment, but I call it discipline. Perhaps there would be fewer kids in jail, on drugs, dropping out, etc., had there been more spankings and backhands every now and then.

My family did not regularly attend church, but we grew up with Godly principles, and prayer was an important part of the fabric of our lives. We were a middle class family, and when I reached the age of five we moved to Prince George's County, Maryland because there began to be more crime in the neighborhood and we needed more space. Six people using one-and-a-half bathrooms was pretty hectic on a weekday morning. We welcomed the larger home and extra bathroom. We felt like the Jeffersons, *Moving on up.* My father worked two full-time jobs to provide for us. By day he worked as a custodian at a local elementary school, and by night he was a Capitol police officer for the federal government. He had a strong work ethic and impressed upon us the importance of working hard. I did not have to look for love from boys or perverted men because my father was present and showed me what real love was. My father was quite witty and was always telling jokes or pulling pranks.

My mother worked full-time at the Department of Housing and Urban Development and religiously cooked six days a week. We always had dinner at 7 p.m. and we eagerly awaited the arrival of our father who came home between jobs. It was then we would share about our day and connect as a family. Our parents poured everything they had into us: all of their wisdom, resources and time. My mom was the more serious one who would help write our school speeches as we ran for class president and other leadership positions in various organizations. She was very prim and proper, a warm and loving soul who always offered a helping hand to those in need. If the television show *Scandal* had been out back then, she would have been known as "The Fixer."

My mother problem-solved for us, her friends, eleven siblings and anyone else who would let her. That was her gift. She purchased a piano so we could learn how to play and be well rounded. I also think she wanted to live vicariously through us because she played the piano as a child. There was not a surplus of money in the household for extra-curricular activities with 11 siblings. However, she was determined to give us every opportunity that was not afforded to her. Success was all we knew in academics, sports, in various talent shows and competitions. She also instilled in us a strong work ethic, the power of faith in ourselves and more importantly, God. We lived by Philippians 4:13, "I can do all things through Christ Jesus who strengthens me."

Every now and then the spirit would move my mother to play her one hit wonder, "Is Your All on the Altar" out of the Baptist hymnal. She couldn't read the bass clef so she would hit the same keys repetitively over and over again while chording the treble clef.

But when it really got good to her, she would begin to sing, pausing intermittently while trying to find the right chord. The strange thing was this usually happened when my siblings and I were watching television. She would eventually stop when we started howling like coyotes, hinting that she was killing our ears. Nevertheless it was her love for music that ignited my passion. The funny thing is that I wasn't born when she purchased the piano. However, of the four children, I was the one who mastered it.

Like Job in the bible, I had a pure heart for God and at an early age. Job was a righteous man, which in plain terms signifies he was not perfect but had a pure heart for God (Job 1:1). He would later be offered up by God to be in the hands of Satan with a promise that he could touch everything but not his soul. In no way am I suggesting that I am perfect; in fact, I'm a long way from perfect. However, I can emphatically say I had a heart for God since childhood that continued through my adult life.

When most little girls played with dolls, my favorite pastime was playing church. I would be the choir director, the preacher, and the pastor's wife, which included wearing one of my mother's hats and waving a hand towel representing a dainty handkerchief. For some odd reason, I always wanted to be a preacher's wife but never the preacher. God was shaping me for ministry even then.

I can remember in elementary school kids would often tease me by singing, "Cynthia's going to heaven" repeatedly. I can still hear that silly song in my head today. The mere fact they knew it would hurt my feelings, meant they would without notice begin to sing that dreadful song whenever I was within earshot. Tears would stream down my face as I declared, "I'm not going to heaven!" I wanted to go to hell with my friends because they made hell look much cooler. I didn't realize that having someone say you were going to heaven was the greatest compliment anyone could receive. But it certainly did not feel like one.

I usually was the last one selected to be on a team during recess and was in the sixth grade before I mastered double-dutch, which simply is jumping with two ropes simultaneously. It took timing and skill. No one was willing to make the effort to teach me how at school. It was like either you were born with the skills or not.

My grade school years were spent being a model student who almost never got into trouble and certainly wasn't sent to the principal's office. They were also spent learning who my true friends were and what real friendship looked like.

My Job Experience

The Teen Years

My teen years would prove to be the beginning of my experience with God and transformation. Maturity happens at different ages for teens. Personally I was very mature and exhibited a lot of wisdom to be so young.

My seventh grade year was a pivotal point in my life. One Sunday morning after an inspiring sermon, I found myself of my own volition walking to the front of the church giving my hand to the preacher and my heart to God. The distance from my chair to the front of the church seemed a mile away; yet somehow I kept moving forward as curious eyes watched my every step. I do not remember having any feelings. It was like being in a trance thinking to myself, *What are you doing?*

I was baptized at the age of 12 at Paramount Baptist Church in Washington, D.C. under the leadership of the Rev. Dr. Ishmael L.

Shaw. By the age of 13, I was singing in the Youth choir, playing and directing the choirs in my stockings, pumps and fully made up in Fashion Fair foundation before there was Bobbi Brown or Mac. Of course I accented with red lipstick. The girls at church talked about me because they said I thought I was better than they were. In reality, I was just more mature and did not believe in playing in church. I wanted to hear the sermon!

I will never forget the day of my true conversion. You see I thought baptism meant to never curse in the *white pants* I was baptized in. But then it happened. On a Wednesday morning before school, televangelist Jim Baker extended an invitation to salvation and I knelt by my bed in front of a thirteen-inch black and white television set. I know that Jim and Tammy Baker have a blemished past in ministry, but the fact still remains that they were the conduit for my true conversion experience. The lesson in this is it is not about the messenger but the message.

In high school, my Sunday school teachers, Mrs. Harvey and Mrs. Taylor would often afford me the opportunity to teach the class, and I would readily do so. I would teach bible study at my house for my friends. I was bold with my faith and had no problem with correcting my peers at church and at school. This Jesus walk was real to me.

In 1985 at the age of 16, I lost my father to a short battle with lung cancer. He was a chain smoker. Smoking was the vice he used to keep himself awake with all the long hours he worked, sometimes 80 plus if he worked overtime. We would beg him to stop smoking as we would ride in the car with windows rolled up in the winter months, getting out smelling like a smoke stack. We were used to holding our breaths and breathing through our mouths.

My dad was a loving father who faithfully came home to his family and provided for us. He ensured that all four of his children would have the resources to go to college. On Saturdays while working on the car, he would teach me the names of various tools ensuring I would not become a helpless woman. He patiently waited for me many mornings to drive me to school as I raced around the house looking for the mate to my shoe. My father allowed me to drive, without a license of course, played silly games and made us laugh uncontrollably with his clichés and funny jokes. Even though I knew he was dying, no one could have prepared me for the pain when he did. It was my first experience with loss. There was nothing I could do but endure the pain and continue to live—that's it and that's all.

That's a message within itself. The Christian is not exempt from pain. Jesus said, "In this world you will have trouble" (John 16:33 New International Version). The question is how will you choose to deal with the pain. Should you just lay down and die? Or should you declare, "I will not die but live to declare the works of the Lord" (Psalm 118:17). I chose to live. What about you? Did you allow the pain to take you out or push you to fulfill your purpose? The choice is up to each of us.

Can you imagine the pain and agony Job must have felt not so much after losing his oxen and asses, then his sheep and camels within minutes of each other because those were things and things can be replaced. But suffering the loss of a loved one or loved ones in an untimely fashion can take you out if you are not careful. If possessions were not enough, Job lost his children as well. I can only imagine that every time he took a breath, a servant would come to inform him of another loss, creating indescribable pain. Have you ever been there? Every time you recover from one tragedy here comes another one. I know that pain. No medicine can eradicate the feeling of loss. There are not enough sleep aids, drugs or alcohol to remove the hurt. As devastating as the loss of my father was, it still was not my Job experience.

CHAPTER THREE

The College Years and Beyond

Upon graduating from high school in 1986, I matriculated to Florida Agricultural and Mechanical University in Tallahassee, Florida where I majored in Business Administration. I was sweetly saved. I can recall on Friday nights, when others were partying in the ball room, my roommates and I would be laid out on the altar at Watson Temple Church of God in Christ. In five years of college, I can count on one hand the number of times I missed church. I was serious and intentional about the things of God.

It was during my junior year that God called me to preach. I can remember it as if it were yesterday. It was during Sunday morning worship while collecting the offering, (not the altar call, I might add), but during the busyness of clanging offering plates, people chattering, asking for change, the choir singing and babies crying, I heard a still small voice saying, "Receive my calling, my child. I am calling you into ministry." I told you that I always wanted to be a preacher's wife but not the preacher. God, are you kidding me? I thought surely, I misunderstood what He had said. I emphatically told God that if He had called me into ministry, He needed to confirm it! Be careful what you ask for. That evening the Holy Spirit came upon me and God undeniably confirmed that He had called me into the gospel ministry. It was as if God had sat on me. Every time I tried to get up off of the bedroom floor, the Spirit would slay me again. God was breaking me and confirming my call all at the same time. My roommates gave an account that as they ran to see what the ruckus was all about, they were met with a supernatural force that prevented them from entering the room even though the door was wide open. I felt like I had been in a tornado. You know tornados don't last long, but while you are in it, it feels like an eternity. I felt like I had been wrestling with an angel like Jacob (Genesis 32:22-32). I felt beat up, but relieved all at the same time. I know it sounds strange, but if you have ever had an intense encounter with God, you know what I am talking about. It is an experience you will never forget. They don't come often but when they come, they have a lasting effect. Needless to say, I submitted to His will.

After refusing a job offer to work as a pharmaceutical sales representative and the opportunity to make six figures, I graduated from Florida Agricultural and Mechanical University May 1991. I accepted a full time job as Minister of Music/Youth at Paramount Baptist Church, where I grew up, making a whopping $18,000 per year. It wasn't a lot of money, but I was working where I was passionate. I loved kingdom work and having an impact on other people's lives.

Pastor Ishmael Shaw was still pastoring at the church and quickly informed me that he would not have "jackleg" preachers on his staff. A "jackleg" is defined as a person who lacks skill and training. Seminary was the furthest thing from my mind. I had never considered it as an option until my conversation with Pastor Shaw. All I knew was that I had a calling on my life to preach. With Pastor Shaw's guidance and support, I subsequently enrolled in Howard University pursuing a Master of Divinity degree. I remember walking through the hallowed halls of Rankin Chapel where I encountered an older conscious, "righteous" sister name Deborah. She wore braids and African garments all the time. I guess she could see how young and green I was. I can clearly recall that day. She said, "Sistahhhhhh hold on to your Jesus." What? Hold on to my Jesus? Where was He going? *I've been saved over ten years and he hasn't left me yet*, I thought to myself. But I would soon learn.

In the fall of 1991, tragedy struck again. My mother was diagnosed with breast cancer. I was trying to make sense of it all. God, this isn't fair! I can recall sitting in Systematic Theology with Dr. Davis and grappling with the age-old question, "If God is good, why does He allow bad things to happen to good people?" My mother was a good person. What about the mothers who have abandoned their children or chose their boyfriends or careers over their children? Why my mother? Wasn't the loss of my father enough?

Systematic theology ideally ties in all the clues from scripture to give the reader a better understanding of who God is, and how we relate to Him. It helps us to understand what is going on in scripture and how it relates to our lives. It is searching the Bible to find all the verses pertaining to a given topic of study. Then putting all the verses together to understand what God wants us to believe.

With no resolve by the teacher or within myself, I left class declaring, "There's no God, no devil, no heaven and no hell! We are all just here!" For two weeks I refused to go to class and when asked why, I responded, "Dr. Davis, you took my Jesus and did not give Him back to me at the end of class." I then understood Deborah's forewarning. Up until that time, my personal theology had not been challenged. Everyone I knew believed the same thing about God. But suddenly I was amongst people who loved the Lord like I did but had a different perspective of Him. Not good or bad, just different. Deborah's words of caution would inevitably prove to be a lesson for life that no matter what trials or tribulations you may experience, don't let anyone or anything take your Jesus. Who or what experience in life have you allowed to take your Jesus? 2 Timothy 1:12 says, "I know whom I have believed." At the end of the day—Hold on to your Jesus.

All I knew was God, but it would be at Howard University's Divinity School that my beliefs and faith would be tried. During this period, I had many preacher friends that were preaching machines. I was a young and gifted preacher in my own right who just happened to be a woman. I was denied the privilege of preaching in the pulpits of other churches on many occasions and offered the floor to herald the gospel message as the Women's Day guest *speaker* and not the guest *preacher*. But that didn't bother me as long as I got the opportunity to say something for my God. My philosophy was you didn't have to believe in my calling. Just listen to me preach and if you doubted if God called women, you were quickly persuaded differently. I cannot tell you how many times seasoned men and women of God came to me after a sermon and confessed their skepticism of women preachers until after hearing me preach. This is not to be boastful but to simply say that your gifts will make room for you (Proverbs 18:16). To all of my sisters, never feel the need to defend your calling, abilities, giftedness in any arena, preacher or not. Show up, do the work and let it speak for you in the pulpit, boardroom, courtroom, classroom or any other room.

CHAPTER FOUR

The Deacon and
the Preacher

While attending seminary at Howard University School of Divinity, I know for a fact that many preachers would not date me because they were intimidated by my preaching abilities. But that was okay with me. It just made room for my Boaz.

In February 1995, I got re-acquainted with and married my Boaz, Kenneth E. Rioland Jr. We got engaged and jumped the broom within eight months. He was not a preacher at the time, but his love for God drew me like a bee to honey or a thirsty panting deer to water. Because of our short engagement, both of our families were skeptical of whether our marriage would last.

I must share our testimony but preface it by saying, "Don't try this at home." My husband and I both attended Florida Agricultural and Mechanical University in Tallahassee, Florida. We knew of each other but ran in two different circles. While he was partying I was praising. Three years after we graduated from college we bumped into each other at the airport. I had come to Tallahassee to attend my college roommate's 30th birthday party and was returning to Washington, D.C. Ken was just arriving to attend his best friend's wedding. He immediately said, "Cynthia Jackson, weren't you saved in college?" I responded, "Yes." He said, "I am saved now too." I thought to myself, *Praise the Lord, but I am marrying a preacher. In addition you just got saved and I've been saved all my life. Poof, be gone.* We exchanged numbers and began to have casual telephone conversations between D.C. and Florida. I decided that it was time to move on because as I stated before, I was going to marry a preacher.

My mother used to say, "Don't tell a man you are sick because you will never get married." That's what the seasoned saints used to say. One night while talking on the phone I remembered what my mother once said. It's funny how you can remember what your mother told you when it works to your benefit. So here I go... "Ken, I have lupus." There was no response. I was confident that this would be our last telephone conversation after that bit of information. Again I said, "Did you hear me? I have lupus and what do you have to say about that?" in my sassy black Sister Souljah voice. In the "spirit" my hands were on my hips, my head was cocked to the side and my lips were pursed together. He paused and said, "Umm… by His stripes you are healed." Yikes! Did he just put scripture on me? Oh no he didn't! Immediately, my defense wall came tumbling down like the walls of Jericho. Well I am sure you can figure out the rest of this story. Twenty-five years later, in the words of Antwone Fisher, "We're still standing! We're still strong!"

All I knew was if he could speak over my life and bring me down a few notches while taking my breath away—he was the man for me. I was drawn in by his love and passion for God, which meant everything to me. Sisters, don't miss your blessing giving God the criteria for your soulmate because God wasn't through with Deacon Kenneth E. Rioland Jr. If I had gone by what I only knew at the moment, I could have potentially missed out on my blessing!

In 1998 we were blessed with a bouncing baby boy, Kenneth Rioland, III whom we call Trés He is our pride and joy. He was quite ill at birth. After seeing numerous specialists, we received the diagnosis that he had neonatal lupus. There was a lot of stress on our marriage during the early years.

The birth of our son caused my lupus to flare and I could not work. Trés was hospitalized. We had a new home and my husband had an extremely stressful commission-based job as a branch manager at Bank of America. After three years of marriage, we were ready to call it quits. How can two leaders in the church quit on their marriage? A deacon and a preacher. Thankfully, in the absence of a mother and a father, my oldest sister Alva removed the option for me to move back home to Washington, D.C. She didn't make it easy for either of us to walk away. Let me parenthetically say that you need people in your life to hold you accountable and not allow you to make quitting a first option in anything.

My husband had taken a job in Durham, North Carolina and I was packing up to go somewhere in the USA with my son. With our home on the market, Ken came home Labor Day weekend to pick up his last bit of possessions. An old preacher, the late Elder Eddie Nunn, was my husband's barber. Many men went to him for a haircut but often also got a sermon or nuggets of wisdom whether they wanted it or not. While in town, Ken decided to get his hair cut. As my husband recounts, Elder Nunn said, "Boy, that girl wasn't bothering you. You went to D.C. and brought her down here to Tampa, now deal with it!"

We attended church that last Sunday at Trinity Gospel Church. God was speaking through the sermon. It was an emotional service as we said farewell to our church family. At the end of service with tears in both of our eyes, my husband said, "Are you ready to go to Durham?" Excuse me? Did I hear right? With a sigh of relief I emphatically said, "Yes!" God was dealing with Ken that weekend and was teaching me that it's not over until He says it's over. As difficult as that was, it was not my Job experience.

Although it was predicted that I was positioned to be the next female preacher on the "circuit," my family became my ministry and I fell off from the preaching scene. Many of my colleagues remained on the preaching scene, both male and female. Their preaching was powerful, and they had a great following. They had powerful life testimonies, but I had been in church all my life; I had no miraculous testimony to give. I had the conviction that in order for God to use you greatly He had to "bruise you deeply." I felt that overcoming a major trial would lend credence to my preaching.

After relocating to Durham, North Carolina, we immediately joined First Calvary Baptist Church under the leadership of Pastor Fredrick Amos Davis where I served as the full-time Church Business Administrator and leader of the Women's Ministry. My husband was the Couples' Ministry Sunday school teacher and eventually Chair of the Men's Ministry. Even though he tried to live a life of obscurity and let me be the "superstar" as he describes it, God still found him. Little did we know that this would be the place where he would receive his call to the gospel ministry. He was licensed in July 2006 and a year later was ordained and called to pastor a church in a rural town in Virginia.

I often felt left behind by my peers because I chose to serve my family, which I don't regret. In hindsight I probably could have been a great mother, wife and preacher simultaneously if I'd had that push or encouragement. Bishop Vashti McKenzie, National Chaplain of

Delta Sigma Theta Sorority, Inc. and the first African American female bishop in the AME Church wrote in her book, *Woman at the Well*, how she learned to write a sermon while washing dishes and changing diapers. Well I washed dishes and changed diapers but there wasn't a whole lot of sermon writing going on during those years.

I experienced many losses during that season. As I mentioned earlier my husband was ordained and we were called to pastor a church in Virginia in 2007. We were both excited about the call and looked forward to the move from Durham to Virginia. Our first order of business was to sell our home. God had blessed us with a brand new custom built brick home in Durham, and while we hated to leave it, we knew God had called us to minister in Virginia. We were willing to make the sacrifices necessary to answer the call. There was another reason I was looking forward to the move. This church was like home to me. My uncle was the emeritus pastor and it was the church where my grandparents served on what was then called the Deacon and Deaconess Board. My mother and her eleven siblings were all baptized there.

It was while we were putting the house up for sale that we discovered a tax lien. We owed the government for outstanding taxes on my husband's cleaning business. I know this sounds crazy and somewhat irresponsible, but it happened. We couldn't afford to keep the house in Durham and live in Virginia because the small rural Baptist church we were going to pastor could only afford to pay us a small salary.

This was a great loss as well. Not the physical house but what it represented. My husband and I prayed over the lot we wanted. While working in Florida with his cleaning business, I drove by the lot we had prayed for and saw a sold sign. I went in and spoke to the real estate agent who apologized. I called Ken in tears because I was sure that was our lot. When he returned, he came by the job and presented me with a card. As I opened the envelope the card read "Congratulations on your new home." Inside was the receipt for the down payment on the lot we had prayed for. Unbeknownst to me, Ken had asked the real estate agent to hold the lot and when he returned he would make the down payment. So you see, it was not the material house but how my husband worked to get the down payment. Everything I wanted was in the house but I had to leave.

Needless to say my husband and I struggled financially trying to pay both the mortgage in Durham and rent in Virginia since we couldn't sell the house because of the lien. We attempted to rent out the house in Durham, but the renters were delinquent in their payments and eventually left altogether. But God was faithful as we left our beautiful home to live in a double-wide trailer that shook when the winds blew and housed mice in the fall when the crops were harvested. I laugh now, but it wasn't funny then. I could no longer afford to shop at major department stores like Macy's. I found myself shopping at the local Walmart. But by the time I accessorized, no one knew the difference. I've learned it's not about what you are wearing, but how you wear it. Clothes don't make you, you make the clothes. Just because it's not a St. John suit or a pair of red bottom shoes doesn't mean you can't look good.

It was in that small town that we saw God do miraculous things in the lives of the people we had the privilege to pastor. We served faithfully at the church for seven years. The church grew exponentially from 40 members to almost 200. Through the grace of God, we made an impact on the church and in the community. Our personal faith grew, and our marriage was strengthened. Reflecting on those years, perhaps God was preparing *us* for *my* Job experience.

CHAPTER
FIVE

Church Hurt

Serving at that little rural church was one of the greatest times in ministry. We hosted women's conferences in excess of 300 women hailing from North Carolina, District of Columbia and Maryland. We started a business incubator designed to support new and startup companies by providing resources and services at a nominal cost. We also revamped the Community Development Corporation which included a boys and girls camp for underprivileged kids raising over $20,000 a year for the program through grants and donations.

As a church, we attended community forums in support of saving jobs at the local fish plant and The Potomac Supply Company. We were a community church whose doors hung on welcome hinges. Our theme was, "We're More Than a Church; We're Family." I believed it and the congregation did too. I loved those people, even the ones who would give you a little trouble every now then.

Ministry was so exciting. You never knew what was going to happen in worship any given Sunday. One member said she used to sit in her car in the parking lot Sunday mornings not very excited to attend church before we came. The Spirit was always moving. We renovated the church to include screens, new pews, office space and bathrooms. We were a country church with a big city mentality. When hurricane Katrina hit Louisiana, one of our members used his own tractor trailer to take food supplies and clothing there. We collected from surrounding counties and were proud to know that the "little" church on the side of the road had spearheaded that effort.

In October 2015 at the end of seven years, my husband got called to pastor a Baptist church in Chesterfield, Virginia two hours away. It was a difficult decision, but we believed it to be the will of God and His next move. When the church learned of our intended departure, it seemed as if everything went south. Not only was the church disappointed in us for leaving, but half of the community as well.

I will never forget the day I saw one of the leaders of the church in a restaurant. They barely spoke or gave eye contact. Boy did that sting. I guess we both felt betrayed but for different reasons. They felt betrayed because we were leaving, and my husband, and I felt betrayed by them for not supporting us in our next God move. At the going away celebration the church hosted, many church members did not attend. Some spoke and then left. One leader took the opportunity to tell the church, "We're going to make it. We're going to be alright," then proceeded to leave without offering one kind word or reflect on our work as I recall it.

We had celebrated so many others when they received promotions, homes, degrees, etc. Yet the congregation we had celebrated, seemed not to find the grace to reciprocate. It was a tumultuous time. I get it… when you love hard you hurt easily. I was hurt, and the church was hurt. I guess they never thought we would leave. I went through a deep depression because even though God was calling us to serve at another church that country church held a special place in my heart.

To add greater pain, my extended family was hurt that we left the home church. They openly expressed their disapproval of our decision. But this was a God move. Couldn't anyone be happy for us? People grow and move on. It's part of the circle of life. It is not unusual for God to change your plans. You have to pray that you have the faith and obedience to trust God even when you can't trace Him. He told Abraham, "Go from your country, your people and your father's household to the land I will show you" (Genesis 12:1 NIV). What about Simon Peter and his brother Andrew? Jesus said to them, "Follow me, and I will make you fishers of men" (Matthew 4:19). It is just what God does. We felt in our hearts that we had fulfilled our mission. If I had my druthers, I would probably still be there today…but God had other plans.

Upon accepting the new pastorate, my husband stayed in Chesterfield during the week while I remained in the country because our son was in his last year of high school. We did not think it was fair to uproot him his senior year. This forced me to answer questions from the community about our decision to move, succumb to cold looks and snide remarks basically by myself. I would never want to go back to that period in my life. It literally was what I imagine a divorce would be like. I cried a lot, contemplated should I stay and had great stress. I have often heard that time heals all wounds. Well, I am a witness.

Today, we see our former church members a couple of times a year, attend their family events and sometimes stop by their homes just to say hello when in town. We laugh about the good times and all the wonderful things we accomplished as a church family by the grace of God. At the end of the day, we knew that we would always be there for one another. We just had to get over the church hurt.

CHAPTER
SIX

Now What

Once our son had graduated from high school and was settled at Hampton University, it was time to focus on ourselves. My husband quickly made the adjustment of having no child in the home. After all, he had been an exceptional father and made great sacrifices for his wife and family. It was now time for him to "live" and do the things that he wanted to do without feeling like he was neglecting his obligations as a family man. Live? What is that? For eighteen years, everything we said and did centered around our only child. We gladly made sacrifices, attended his basketball and soccer games, robbed Peter *and* Paul to put him through private school and purchased $300 soccer shoes with his name on them for his senior year as captain of the team. We lived to make him happy. Every parent can identify with this. But as a mother, I did not know how to repurpose myself. I was still trying to hold on to a child who was no longer in our home.

Sisters, it is a blessing to be a mother and wife, but that is not our identity. We are more than the maid, chauffeur, cook, church worker, lover and all the other roles we play. There is purpose in each of us and it is incumbent upon us to find that purpose. I have found that when we fulfill one purpose, God moves us to fulfill the next purpose. The problem is that many of us are between purposes twiddling our thumbs saying, "Now what?" Stella, get your groove back! Stop waiting to exhale and EXHALE! I wasted two years lamenting over the fulfilled purpose of raising my child when I could have been moving on to the "next."

My husband said he was no longer parenting but consulting. Now some people might take issue with this statement. But what he was really saying is that we had poured everything we had into that little boy for eighteen years. If he did not have it by now, he would never get it. It is time to act as consultants for him as he makes his own decisions for his life.

After a couple of years of mourning over my son leaving the nest, I enrolled into a doctoral program with an emphasis on Christian Leadership and Spiritual Renewal in the fall of 2017. This was an effort to repurpose myself. I had no more excuses as to why I could not hone my gift of preaching, learn a new skill, find a new ministry or *write a book;* but I was too busy saying, "Now what?" I don't know what your *now what* is, but find it with a quickness because life is too short. My First Lady in Florida, Ariole Nunn used to say, "The only thing worse than a young bitter woman is an old bitter woman!" So I stopped twiddling my thumbs to move towards my future. Are you still sitting on the sidelines of life reliving an old purpose? Stop it! Life is too precious.

In January 2018, I sat across from my mentor Pastor Pamela McLaughlin in Panera Bread. I vividly recall telling her that my colleagues in ministry had strong testimonies, but I did not have one. I had no compelling story of being strung out on drugs, mentally or sexually abused, having a child out of wedlock, homelessness, dysfunctional parents, major illnesses or any significant tragedies to attest to from my perspective. I needed some credence to make my preaching more powerful and credible, so I thought. Sure I had lost two parents and almost ended up divorced, but that was small potatoes compared to what many of my colleagues had endured. Little did I know what was to come. I was about to have my own personal Job experience.

My Job Experience

CHAPTER
SEVEN

My Job Experience

Who hasn't heard of the story of Job? I mean it would be difficult to call oneself a Christian and not know something about him. I think even the unbeliever in some context has heard of him. The Bible declares that he was a wealthy righteous man. He prayed for his children every morning *just in case* they had sinned (Job 1:5).

At some point God and Satan have a conversation about Job. God offers him up with the stipulation that Satan can touch anything belonging to Job except his very life. Job in turn loses his cattle, oxen, camels, servants and all his children through thievery or calamity in a matter of seconds (Job 1:13-19). If that wasn't enough, Job was stricken with painful boils all over his body.

I have read this story hundreds of times, heard this text preached a million times, but it was not until I had my own personal Job experience that I could possibly identify with his suffering. For the first time, I saw this story through different lenses. I would imagine that most of us could identify with Job in some form or fashion.

My Job experience began the week of August 31, 2018. For three days I ran a temperature of 103 degrees. I thought nothing of it, assuming it was some type of virus or flu. But thank God for my cousin Dr. Yvonne Treakle-Moore who was a physician. Two weeks earlier, my neurologist had prescribed a medication to stop my non-epileptic seizures. They were involuntary random movements that lasted about ten seconds, not severe like normal seizures. But it was cause for concern. My body was having a negative reaction to the medication. It was different from an allergy. My cousin was so concerned that she got a doctor's appointment for me that same day because she sensed it was something greater. I couldn't even think enough to call my doctor because the reaction to the medicine made it difficult to use my mental faculties. She said the Spirit arrested her and led her to call me back immediately because she could hear that I was not myself. My thoughts were disjointed, and I was extremely weak. Despite having a fever, I repeatedly complained of being cold. I was fully dressed with three blankets doubled and an electric blanket, but it still didn't do the trick. Did I mention that my cousin lives in Fort Washington, Maryland, and I live in Chesterfield, Virginia? She was able to get a doctor's appointment with another physician because my doctor was on vacation. I am convinced that this was a move of God. Had it not been for her, I would have treated the symptoms not knowing that there was something more gravely wrong.

Isn't that what we often do in life? We treat the symptoms instead of getting to the root of the problem. As God would have it, my spiritual daughter and Armor Bearer, Rosie was off from work and drove me to my doctor's appointment. My husband was on travel for work. When I arrived at the doctor's office I could barely walk. They confirmed my temperature, took a throat culture and I tested positive for strep throat. They immediately sent me to the emergency room at a local hospital where I was admitted. Small dots began to appear on my arms like a rash. As I lay on the bed in the emergency room, I repeatedly asked for a blanket because I was so cold, but I received the response, "Not until your fever breaks."

The next thing I recall clearly was awakening to a team of doctors from the burn unit bandaging my entire body. Yes, the burn unit! Can you imagine having your last memory be in the emergency room of one hospital, only to come to yourself *a week later* in critical care at The Medical College of Virginia Hospital (MCV) and your body looking as if you had been in a fire? I get chill bumps just thinking about it. How did this happen? Why did this happen? This isn't fair! What did I do to deserve this? These were questions that flooded my mind as I stared at the unfamiliar faces that crowded my small hospital room. But it was me who said that I didn't have a real testimony.

Like Job, I felt as if I had been offered up as a sacrifice. I could imagine God saying, "Have you considered my servant Cynthia?" I am in no way suggesting that I am as perfect or righteous as Job. However, I can attest to the fact that I earnestly strive to live a blameless life before God; I always have. That was the point of me telling you about my childhood and early adult years to show how I had served God since my youth. God, are you kidding me? This is what I get in return? The only scripture I could think of was, "That ye may prove to be the children of your Father which is in heaven: for He maketh his sun to rise on the evil and on the good, and sendeth **rain on the just** and on the **unjust [emphasis added]**" (Matthew 5:45). In my opinion, it wasn't just raining—it was pouring. I was about to get a true test and a testimony whether I wanted it or not.

Apparently, the burn unit had been changing my bandages for the past week. There were blisters all over my body, flesh hanging and open wounds. Some were so large that they covered my entire chest and hip. My skin was peeling, lips were swollen, infection was in my mouth, and private areas and wires were everywhere, including a feeding tube, catheter and an incessant amount of morphine being pumped into my system to ease the pain. I would soon learn that I had developed a severe case of Stevens-Johnson Syndrome.

What in the world is that? Stevens-Johnson Syndrome is a rare, serious disorder of the skin and mucous membranes. It usually occurs as a reaction to a medication or an infection. Often it begins with flu-like symptoms, followed by a painful red or purplish rash that spreads and blisters. This definition is simplistic compared to all its effects.

The doctors had prognosticated that I was not going to come out of this sickness; they said that if the syndrome continued to progress, death was eminent. It had begun to attack my liver. My bladder was not passing all its fluids. I began to experience double vision and I literally lost the flesh from my back. My systems began to gradually shut down, but the devil must not have gotten the email, text message, phone call, tweet or notification that "I shall not die but live to declare the works of the Lord" (Psalm 118:17).

My friend, I learned through this experience that God will give you a test like Job to see if you will trust him or "curse God and die" (Job 2:9). I didn't know what I was saying on that cold winter evening while sitting at the table in Panera Bread with my mentor. God, the creator of the universe, the Alpha and Omega, the one who knows the path that we take, will permit a Job experience. It may be financial, spiritual, physical or emotional, but you will have a Job experience and what will be your response? Like Job, mine was "Though He slay me yet will I trust in Him" (Job 13:15).

I had come too far, experienced too much for this to be my end. I had a son to see graduate from college; grandbabies yet to be born to spoil beyond measure; a wonderful husband to grow old with and a ministry and purpose to fulfill. Remember God had given Satan specific guidelines and restrictions pertaining to Job. The enemy knows what his limitations are as it pertains to the children of God. But the question is *"Do you know the limitations the enemy has as it pertains to your life?"* Satan can only go as far as God will allow him to. No matter how dark it gets in your personal life or how great your loss, remember that the enemy has some restrictions and limitations. There is a line drawn in the sand that he *cannot* cross. I wanted to live. I was literally knocking at death's door. Even though I could not pray, I believe the spirit in me was determined to fight. There were some promises to be fulfilled, blessings with Cynthia LaShone Jackson Rioland's name on it, impact to be made through my ministry and certainly no devil in hell was going to block those promises.

If you are in the midst of your personal Job experience—trust Him. If you have just come out of your personal Job experience— praise Him. And if you are about to go into your personal Job experience—hold on to Him. God is with you.

Beloved, there will be times in life when you will not be able to pray for yourself. But I am foolish enough to believe that in that moment when I could not pray, I had some prayers stored up over the years. I was pulling off a reservoir of prayers that had been prayed since I was a little girl. I had a Christian family, church family, and friends who were calling out my name all over the country.

Moreover, I later found out that people were praying for me that I did not know, and did not know me. My name was listed in bulletins of churches that I had never visited, prayer lists of Sororities and Fraternities, prayer groups and friends of friends who touched heaven on my behalf. You never know who is praying for you. Someone just asked them to call out my name. It gave a new meaning to the song, *Somebody prayed for me had me on their mind, took a little time to pray for me.* I am clear that it was the unfailing fervent effectual prayers of the righteous that brought me through and the mercy of God" (James 5:16).

So often people ask for prayer and we assure them that we are going to call out their name but never do. I mention this because when people request prayer, we must be intentional in remembering to lift their names up. Our prayers are the conduit by which people get healed, delivered and set free. We casually call people's names out (if we remember to do so). Don't just pray for yourself, someone's spiritual and or physical life is dependent upon your prayer. We never know when we are going to need prayers reciprocated. In my time of crisis, I needed someone to call out my name because I could not do it for myself. Who is waiting and depending on your prayer to make it through the next day or even tonight?

Of all the people that came to visit and pray for me that first week, I can only recall Bishop Anthony G. Maclin and Lady Peggy Maclin of the Sanctuary at Kingdom Square in Capital Heights, Maryland. With all of the morphine in my system, I was lucid enough to recognize and remember their visit for some odd reason.

When they heard I was ill, they traveled over two hours to pray for me. As Bishop recounted, when he got to the critical care unit and saw I was in the corner room, he knew it was time for spiritual warfare. He later told me that I was the third person that month who was fighting for their life that he had prayed over. Each of us coincidentally, or maybe not, were placed in the corner room. I asked Bishop what was significant about the corner room. His response was chilling. He said that generally when the hospital staff thinks you are not going to make it, they put you in the corner room—away from everyone else.

How many of you have ever been put in the corner room? I am not necessarily talking about in the hospital, but the corner room of life where people have given up on you or thought you could not make it out, make it over or make it through! But I am here to encourage you; just because they put you in the corner room does not mean that you cannot or will not make it out.

In the boxing arena, there is something called "the corner man." In general, a corner man is a person who is permitted to be present in a fighter's corner during a boxing match in order to provide advice or assistance to the fighter. Okay here it is...I made it out because I had a "corner man" named Jesus Christ. "The stone the builders rejected has become the cornerstone" (Psalm 118:22).

My Job Experience

What's in You
Will Come Out of You

While attending Florida Agricultural and Mechanical University (FAMU) I participated in the prestigious FAMU Gospel Choir. We would travel across the state of Florida, the Virgin Islands and even up north during spring break. We spent many weekends on the road performing at various churches. One weekend we had an engagement in St. Petersburg, Florida. With approximately 75-100 members, we traveled in cars during a literal monsoon. We could barely see. There were five of us traveling in my car. Sherwood, our director, was driving, Becky was in the passenger seat, my roommate Sherry, Madelyn and I sat in the back. Madelyn was sweetly saved. She wore thick glasses, a Jheri curl and long skirts. Madelyn very rarely had anything to say.

The three of us were sound asleep in the back seat during the storm. Due to a visual impairment and the downpour, Sherwood slammed on the brakes. Sherry and I jerked forward in our seats and screamed "Jesus!" Madelyn on the other hand yelled, "Oh S—!" Immediately there was an awkward silence. We shared a look of shock, followed by uncontrollable laughter. Who knew Madelyn had that in her?

What's the point of this story? What's in you will come out of you. It's when life slams on the brakes that we find out what's really in us. While I have no recollection of this, my husband said that even though I was heavily sedated, he could hear me repeatedly saying, "Jesus, Jesus, Jesus," in a still small voice! Even in a subconscious state, my spirit man called on the only one who could help me.

My friend, a Job experience has a way of bringing out of you what's in you. May I ask, "What's really in you?" Is it fear or faith? Worry or worship? Panic or praise? Doubt or determination? Don't wait until you are in the midst of your Job experience to realize what is in you. Just because you are a preacher, sing in the choir, attend Sunday school, serve in the usher ministry or any other ministry within the church does not mean that you have what it takes to go through your Job experience. Job had intense conversations with God, friends suggested that he had sinned, Mrs. Job said curse God and die. He had lost possessions and family. His body was racked with pain. Yet with all these interferences internally and externally, from within the deepest part of his belly, Job's trust and faith rested in God and God alone. Throughout the Book of Job, intermittently woven in, are numerous affirmations of his trust in God and praise for the creator because that is what was in Job (Job 1:21, Job 13:15, Job 23:10).

So again I ask, "What's in you?" Only you can answer that question. If all that's in you is hell, bitterness, unforgiveness and doubt, you will never make it through your Job experience. If Naomi had stayed bitter, she would have never deposited into Ruth. If the woman with the issue of blood was full of doubt, she would have never gotten healed. This is not a rhetorical question. I challenge you to search your heart and ask God to give you everything you need to go through. Tell God to fill you with His strength, joy, peace and His word.

As I struggled to learn how to walk again, I would recite with conviction Philippians 4:13, "I can do all things through Christ who strengthens me." I called alive the word of God that I preached about and read about. I recited Isaiah 53:5b and made it personal, "By his stripes I am healed." I recited every scripture I could think of that could get me through my Job experience. What's in you? Do you have what you need? Do you have what it takes? I found inside of me unknown strength and courage. My husband repeatedly stated how proud he was of me. He said that he didn't know I had it in me. Shucks, I am proud of myself because I would have never thought I had it in me to move beyond this experience.

I am not sure which was hardest, the syndrome itself or the recovery process. When I had to go to the restroom, I would try on my own to get out of the bed. There was purpose in me and purpose could not be fulfilled lying in the bed with tubes all over the place while having a pity party. I thought about the little song, "Rise Sally rise, wipe your weeping eyes." I am not saying that I didn't cry, but for every tear there was a press to move forward.

Well, I have asked you repeatedly, "What's in you?" No one can answer this question but you. I challenge you to dig down deep as I prophetically speak over you—GIRLFRIEND, YOU GOT IN YOU EVERYTHING YOU NEED TO MAKE IT OUT! I found faith, prayer, courage, strength and the word of God.

CHAPTER NINE

What Are You Holding on to?

You may recall me mentioning a feeding tube in earlier chapters and that the syndrome had affected my systems, which included my digestive system. On numerous occasions, the nursing staff or visitors would inadvertently pull my feeding tube which was surgically placed inside my stomach. I cannot possibly articulate the kind of pain experienced whenever the tube was pulled because it was stitched to my inner nostrils and then flowed to a bag full of nutrients designed to sustain me. I became so paranoid that I would literally tense up when the nurses came to check my vital signs and change my IV.

I could not eat because my mouth was infected with thrush. Thrush is a white coating or white patches on the tongue, mouth, inner cheeks, and the back of the throat. The lesions are extremely painful.

My sisters Alva and Gladys, who stayed with me for a while and my husband would remind the staff ever so gingerly to watch out for the feeding tube. Without fail and despite the friendly reminder someone would ultimately yank the tube which would send me into a frenzy. The feeding tube was surgically placed inside me the first week. Of course I have little to no recollection of this because of the heavy sedation. Gladys and Alva said that I kept tugging at the tube with the hopes of pulling it out. It was clear that it was extremely uncomfortable. The staff suggested tying my hands down. But thank God for my sisters and my husband who suggested hand mitts and a promise that they would ensure I would not pull the feeding tube out.

My sisters said that I would work relentlessly trying to pull the hand mitts off in a futile attempt to remove the feeding tube. Remember that I was *heavily* medicated at this point. Gladys and Alva said that it would take about an hour of hard work and determination before I would get one mitt off. This was no small feat in my estimation. They would put the mitt back on and the process started all over again.

About midway through the week, my sister Gladys came up with the idea of giving me something to hold on to. The staff suggested a small pink pillow that I kept after leaving the hospital.

Whenever I would become agitated by the annoying feeding tube, she would place the pink pillow in my hand. She would ask, "Do you want your pink pillow?" With a faint "um hm" from me, she would gently place it in the palm of my hand, and almost immediately I would calm down. Everyone was amazed including the staff at how holding on to that small pink pillow seemed to offer great comfort. It didn't seem like much to them, but it was everything to me.

When you are going through your crisis or your Job experience what or who do you hold on to? Is it the assurance of the wealth of money in your bank account? You do know that money gets funny and change gets strange. Is it the assurance of your boo thing until he no longer wants to be "booed up?" Perhaps it's your education or experience. I hate to disappoint you by bursting your bubble, but you need something, or should I say someone who is sure to hold on to.

The Holy Spirit, like my little pink pillow, is a comforter in the time of need. You see the pink pillow did not change my situation, but it comforted me in my situation. In fact, the feeding tube remained in place for the entire stint of my hospital stay. The pink pillow did not serve as a means for removing the feeding tube, but it helped me to endure the feeding tube. Beloved, the Holy Spirit is who we need to hold on to when we become agitated by our current status. You may ask, "Who is the Holy Spirit?"

As believers we know that Holy Spirit is not a thing but a person. The Holy Spirit is a real person who came to reside within Jesus Christ's true followers after Jesus rose from the dead and ascended to heaven. The Holy Spirit is a comforter. Comforter means literally having someone to rock you in the cradle of their arms and to wipe your tears away. The Greek word for Holy Spirit is *parakletos* which translates to several things. It means advocate, intercessor, legal assistant and in this case "called to one's aid." Over time it has also been translated to mean to "comfort or console." The same way that pillow brought comfort, the Holy Spirit brings comfort to our souls. Hold on to the Comforter.

CHAPTER
TEN

The "Gift" That Keeps on Giving

When you read about Job's loss, you learn that he did not have the opportunity to recover from one loss before he was notified of the next. I can imagine Job wondering, *When will it all stop*? That is where I found myself. The Stevens-Johnson syndrome had one turn after another. I mockingly referred to it as the "gift" that keeps on giving.

I naively thought that it was all over once I left the hospital and it was now time to heal, but that wasn't the case. The skin on my hands and feet began to harden. I would spend hours on end picking my hands, annoyed at the fact that I had little to no sensory. The skin was so thick that my iPhone did not recognize my touch identification for logging into applications.

The next "gift" was that my fingernails and toenails began to shed. My fingernails took several months to grow back; however, my toenails took almost a year. It was difficult to wear shoes because my toenails were lifting as they were growing out with a new separate nail coming in. I handled all of this fairly well.

I then started noticing that whenever I combed my hair it came out by the handful. It is one thing to wear a wig or weave because you want to and another thing when you wear it because you must. Admittedly, this was one of the hardest things about my Job experience. A woman's hair is her glory (1 Corinthians 11:15). Every African-American sister knows the importance of keeping her hair "whipped." It is the reason why we go to the hairdresser every other week and pay an exorbitant amount of money; it's so that someone can compliment us on our hair. You can look a hot mess, but if your hair is "whipped," no one sees the raggedy shoes, sweat pants and tank top. I need every sister to support me on this one.

My appearance has always been important to me. But during that time my nails were no longer polished, my hair was reduced to strands and my entire face and body were scarred. The only word I could think of to describe my state during that time was broken. The things that I prided myself on were gone. There was nothing left to hide behind. I would just sit in the bathroom looking in the mirror as silent tears ran down my cheeks. The tears were silent because I had wept so much there was no voice left in me. I can better

54

understand why Hannah lay at the altar where the only thing she could do was move her lips (1 Samuel 1:13).

By divine intervention, I found a Christian hairdresser near my home who worked with natural hair. Each week I sat in her chair contemplating cutting off the final strands left. Melanie would say, "Whenever you're ready." All I had were two thin braids about a quarter of an inch thick and I was totally bald on the sides. Those two braids somehow gave me the false sense of security I needed to get out of the bed each morning. For four months or more I religiously went to get my hair washed and braided. Melanie never pushed me even though we both knew it was time to let the old go so the new could come in. She waited until I was ready.

It was in late January or February 2019 before I got the courage to let it go. I was finally ready to accept my reality that I was practically bald. You see you have to let go of the old before the new can come in. Like Melanie my hairdresser, God graciously allows us to keep coming to him week after week. He knows what we need to let go of, but being the kind God that He is, He patiently waits until we are ready.

What is it that you need to let go of so the new can come in? Is it hurt, your past, fear, unforgiveness, self-righteousness? I would contend that all of us have something to let go of. The truth of the matter is God cannot do a new thing in you until you let the old go

(Isaiah 43:18-19). Is today your day? Is right now as you read this book the moment to let it go? Only you can make that decision.

To add pain to misery, my back was the last thing to heal. The gift that kept on giving left large keloids all over my back and chest. They will never go away. Keloids are the result of the skin healing too fast. Twice a day the nurses or my husband would put oil over my entire body. Never did I ever dream that my healing would include keloids.

Trying to accept my new normal seemed to be more than I could bear and it was, and some days it still is. Through much prayer and a husband who tells me regularly that I am still beautiful, I continue to carry on. It is funny how days when I struggle with my looks, God sends someone to reaffirm me. Just recently I went through the drive through at Chick-fil-A and the cashier stopped and said, "Excuse me, miss, but you are so beautiful." God knew what I needed on that day. As women we must learn that true beauty is from the inside and not the outside. We can get all made up, but if we have an ugly spirit, that is what permeates through. The bible declares that, "Charm is deceptive, and beauty is fleeting; but a woman who fears the LORD is to be praised" (Proverbs 31:30 NIV).

God is not in the business of taking us through just to take us through. He wants us to learn something about Him, ourselves and life. Through my Job experience I learned what is really important. Society puts so much emphasis on appearance. What if we cared about our spirit man as much as we care about our physical man? As women, we spend money on our hair, nails and clothing and then have the unmitigated gall to say we don't have money to buy a book to enhance our lives or money to attend a conference that will enrich our spirits. We must change our perspective and change our priorities.

There were other "gifts" Stevens-Johnson gave that I'd rather not mention. But during a time of reflection I came to the realization that I had received another gift that superseded them all. It was not from Stevens-Johnson; it was from God. It was the gift of life because I am not supposed to be here. The gift was *God's Grace and Mercy.*

My Job Experience

CHAPTER ELEVEN

It's Only a Moment

Second Corinthians 4:17 says, "For our light affliction, which is but for a moment, worketh for us a far more exceeding weight of glory." Five weeks later, as I sat on my bed at the rehabilitation center, I said to my friend, Rev. Pamela McLaughlin, "It seems like only a moment." Immediately my spirit leaped. I had come to the realization that all I had been through was just a moment in the grand scheme of things. Yes, I still had scars as proof of what I had been through, but on the other side of "through" it seemed as if it was a distant memory.

Let me be honest and say that when I was in the midst of it all, it felt like an eternity. But when I came out on the other side, it seemed as if it was only a moment. Merriman-Webster dictionary defines the word moment as a minute portion or point of time. Moments have a beginning and an ending, my friend. Older saints would say that trouble don't last always. When you put your affliction or Job experience in proper context, it is only a moment compared to what we gain eternally. What you are experiencing now can only last but so long. Hang on in there. God has put something inside of you to endure whatever challenges you may be facing. The Greek word for moment is translated as "too small to be measured." Whew! When I got that revelation, I started to think about others in the Bible. The woman had the issue of blood for a moment. Daniel was in the lion's den for a moment. The three Hebrew boys were in the fiery furnace for a moment. Joseph was in prison for a moment. What they gained from their momentary affliction was far greater than the length of time of suffering and the degree of loss.

We never know what life will present us with, but remember there is a time limit on your affliction. My mother used to say, "It won't always be this way." I didn't understand it then, but my mother had the right perspective. Do you have the right perspective?

While lying in the hospital bed, I had no choice. Like Job, I had to wait for my change to come and I looked forward to returning back to my life, not as I knew it, but better, stronger and wiser. After all, what is the point of enduring afflictions if you don't glean something to benefit you? You may not see it now, but your afflictions are working something for your good. I don't know what it is, but time will tell. Furthermore, it will make what you went through worth your while. The bible says Job got double for his trouble once he prayed for his friends (Job 42:10).

I cannot tell you when your Job experience will end, but tell yourself it is only for a moment. The Apostle Paul said, "And after you have suffered a little while, the God of all grace, who has called you to his eternal glory in Christ, will himself RESTORE, confirm, strengthen, and establish you." (1 Peter 5:10 English Standard Version). Let God do His perfect work. Remember it is only for a moment.

My Job Experience

CHAPTER
TWELVE

Mary Did You Know?

We live in a very quaint older neighborhood in Chesterfield, Virginia. Most of the neighbors' children are grown and have gone off to college or to write the next chapter of their lives. Throughout the day, you will see people jogging or walking their dogs. It is in this context that we know a few of our neighbors. My husband Ken walks our Pomeranian Polo every morning. Every now and then when I can let the sheets go, I will also walk with him.

You can almost assuredly count on running into Betty, a cancer survivor and Mary, the "Neighborhood watch" or better yet "Mrs. Kravitz" of the late '70s TV show hit, *Bewitched*. She is the one who knows about everything that is going on in the neighborhood. Mary is an older woman, probably in her late sixties or early seventies. She loves being sociable and engaging the various residents. While we enjoy talking with Mary, our conversations over the past three years have been very light and limited.

After not seeing me for a while and seeing less of Ken because he was staying at the hospital, Mary and Betty began to make inquiries. Ken shared that I was extremely ill in the hospital and it would be a while before I would come home. Mary and Betty are very pleasant and are part of the few people we know by name in the community. They always showed great concern and conveyed their prayers for me throughout my illness.

Upon returning home, Ken and I were going to a follow-up appointment. There at the entry of our subdivision was none other than Mary taking her morning stroll. I was so excited to speak to her, so I rolled down the window on my side and exclaimed, "Hi, Mary." Mary with her shades on responded, "Excuse me?" I said, "Mary, it's me." She said, "I'm sorry and you are?" My protective husband quickly leaned forward around me and upon seeing him she connected the dots.

What was amazing was her response after realizing it was me. It went something like this, "Oh Cynthia, you poor girl. You're going to get better. Oh, my goodness. You poor girl." Then she began to diplomatically explain why she didn't recognize me, but I knew the truth. She couldn't see beyond my scars. I wasn't offended, but her response reminded me of the drastic change I had gone through. It was true I had dark spots on my face and my lips were somewhat swollen and disfigured, but the preaching moment was that she had no idea of how far I had come.

There are times in life when people will feel pity for you, but if they only knew how far you had come and what you had endured, their response would be totally different. I wanted to say, "Mary, did you know that it was prognosticated that I would not make it?" "Mary, did you know that these are healing scars that were once literally open wounds?" "Mary, did you know about the feeding tube, the layers of skin that fell from my body, the swollen lips and sores in my mouth?" But Mary didn't know. She could only see where I was now. She meant no harm, I am sure, in her response. After all, I wasn't the beautiful, well-put-together young lady she would often see in the neighborhood walking the dog with my husband.

I was the type of person who even when walking my dog made sure my winter hat, gloves and coat matched. In the spring, I would dress in bright colors full of cheer and vitality. But now Mary didn't recognize me. If only she could have seen where I came from, my progress and great feats against the odds, perhaps she would have rejoiced with me and not pitied me.

When people don't personally witness what you have been through, how can you expect them to appreciate where you are? How often have we stood in judgment of others without knowledge of the afflictions they have endured, whether mental, spiritual or physical. I had scars—not wounds! There is a difference. Wounds are the signs of an injury, but scars are the sign of healing. There is a quote by Craig Scott who said, "From every wound there is a scar, and every scar tells a story. A story that says, I survived."

Mary saw wounds, but I saw scars. They serve as a constant reminder of what you have been through and how you prevailed. They tell your story. You may recall in Genesis 32:22-32 where Jacob wrestled with the angel all night long. When it was all over, the angel hit Jacob in the thigh in order to be released from his grip. From that point on, Jacob had a limp for the rest of his life. We could feel sorry for Jacob that he had a limp or rejoice because it meant he had prevailed. When I see my scars and want to be down, I remind myself that I prevailed over the circumstance by the grace and mercy of God.

So, my friend, if you have scars, celebrate the fact that you made it through, over, under or around your affliction. Every soldier that has endured combat will have a scar or two so that when people ask, "How did you get that scar?" You can emphatically share your testimony.

I am confident that after all of Job's boils had healed, he had scars. Job 2:7-8 tells us that he had boils from the soles of his feet to the top of his head. He took cut pieces of pottery to scrape his boils to gain relief as he sat in ashes, a sign of mourning. Medically speaking you do not want to burst boils because they have found that they in fact leave scars. Like Job, I had boils that oozed with puss from the soles of my feet to the top of my head. The doctors wanted to drain them surgically, but some of the boils burst on their own, which created greater scars. Ironically, the areas that give me the greatest discomfort are where I had boils the size of an orange or larger.

As I go through the healing process, it has created great discomfort. Sometimes it feels like I have fallen into a bed of red ants and can find no comfort. Through potent cortisone creams, pills and painful injections, I remind myself I am healing. So, don't become down with the "Marys" you will encounter in your healing process. Mary does not know. How could she? She wasn't there.

My Job Experience

That's What Friends Are For

D o you remember the song, "That's What Friends Are For"? I loved the version by Dionne Warwick, Elton John, Gladys Knight, and Stevie Wonder. As I reflect on the wonderful and thoughtful things friends did for me, I can't help but think of this all-time hit. It is not until you go through a crisis that you find out who your real friends are.

When Job was afflicted, his three friends: Eliphaz, Bildad and Zophar came to console him. For seven days they sat upon the ground with him (Job 2:13). This is what I call the ministry of presence. It is simply being available to listen to and support someone in need. Words are not always necessary. It is just knowing that someone is there with you. When my father passed away my mother often spoke of her friend who came over every day for several months because my mom didn't like being alone. She said there was comfort in knowing that someone was nearby. The value of the ministry of presence is often overlooked or under appreciated.

When I was ill, Rosie came every day for six weeks after work and sat with me. I could probably count on one hand how many words Rosie spoke, but it was very comforting to know someone was there. It allowed my husband to take care of business and work without worries. For some reason—please don't judge me—but the song "Tennessee Whiskey" seemed to console me in an unusual way. It was Rosie's ringtone and I just liked the song. I don't think I've listened to that song since. Every now and then I would ask Rosie to play "Tennessee Whiskey." This was so odd because I don't necessarily care for country music, but something about the transition of chords soothed my soul.

Where Job's friends went wrong is that they began to pontificate on why Job was in the predicament he was in. Their justification for Job's mishap was that it was punishment for some sin in his life. I am confident that this is not what Job needed to hear in the midst of his pain and agony. His three friends were convinced that no one suffers innocently and they advised him to ask for God's forgiveness (Job 8). In Job chapter 42, the Lord rebuked Job's friends because they had not spoken truth.

I am grateful for the many friends who were there for me during my time of need. I will not call them all by name, but I will mention the many acts of kindness I received in an effort to show what true friendship looks like. Marquita cleaned my house so when my sisters arrived in town it would be presentable. I don't know if I would have thought of doing something like that. Two of my high school friends Jaynell and Veonca were alarmed when they received an ambiguous email from a family member to pray. These two ladies who do not drive out of town very often got in the car on a Sunday morning after a hurricane to find me. They were determined to see me even though I was not receiving visitors. The beauty of it was that they didn't know what hospital I was in and purposed that they would go to every hospital from Richmond to Chesterfield until they found me. As God would have it, on their first try, they found me.

Words could never express the feeling of gratitude for the sacrifice and determination displayed. It was a dreary cloudy day and everyone was at church, but God sent them to comfort me. They were like a ray of sunshine. I will never forget it as long as I live. Even talking about it brings tears to my eyes to this day.

To my chagrin, I found myself in the hospital for my 50th birthday. I had planned a big celebration, with invitations, menu and entertainment. Even though I was in the hospital, my dear husband made sure there was a celebration. He had a birthday cake and sandwiches delivered. One of my girlfriends went to the store and purchased earrings and a gown to fit over my bandages. She brushed my hair and made me as presentable as possible. A couple of my aunts and uncles drove into town to celebrate with me, but what blessed me even more was that one of my best friends Lynn, drove from Connecticut by herself to be with me on that special day.

Another bestie, Kim stayed a night in rehab and later took off from work to stay with me while my husband had to go out of town. She took me to my follow-up doctor's appointments and when I lost my hair brought a hairstylist in from Washington, D.C. to make me a custom wig.

True friends do not have to talk every day. They just need to be there when you need them. Another friend who I did not talk to often purchased me a rollator so I could get around until my legs got stronger. Perhaps you may not see the value in these acts of kindness, but I guarantee you that all of us at some point or another will need a friend. Not just a friend but a *true* friend who will stick with you through the thick and the thin.

Some sisters have convinced themselves that they are self-sufficient and don't need friends. I don't believe that. God created us to be relational. What I do believe is that perhaps these individuals have been hurt by so-called friends and finally decided "If that's how friends treat you, I don't need one." If you tell yourself something long enough you will begin to believe it.

I will admit that maintaining relationships is not my greatest strength. But I am grateful for every friend who stayed connected to me even when I didn't reciprocate that same commitment. These are true friends who love you in spite of yourself. They know your imperfections, frailties and idiosyncrasies but still love you through your dysfunction, pain and fears.

Some past friendships were destroyed because of third parties with hidden agendas. I must own up to that. Other friendships were compromised because I wouldn't use my voice to express my hurts. Then there have been friendships where it seemed like I was doing all the giving and sharing. As a word of advice, if you give them a pearl and they don't give you one back, newsflash…they really aren't your friend.

This sickness made me realize how important friendships are. I have two cousins, Monique and Michelle, who are like best friends and I may have at some juncture convinced myself that between them and my two sisters, I had enough friends. But this experience has taught me that there are people in addition to them who genuinely love me for who I am and are willing to take the steps necessary to maintain that relationship. The bible declares in Proverbs 18:24a (American King James Version), "A man that has friends must show himself friendly."

Since this illness I have made the commitment to let go of past hurts experienced in friendships, reconnect with those I went offline with, and ask for forgiveness for those I have hurt. As much as you try to let go, a real friend will not let you go. With all of Job's friend's faults, the revelation was that they were there in chapter 2, but they were also there in chapter 42. Translation: Real friends will be with you in the beginning and at the end. Maya Angelou said, "People will forget what you said. People will forget what you did, but people will never forget how you made them feel."

CHAPTER FOURTEEN

He Was There
All the Time

I told you about my wonderful husband. He is an amazing father, provider and protector. I have always appreciated him but never like now. We travel around the country facilitating couple's conferences disseminating information on what a godly marriage looks like. We took vows before God and man. Part of which states, "in sickness and health; for richer or poorer."

This short chapter is dedicated to my partner in life and ministry. He was there! For six weeks he spent every night at the hospital. Can you imagine being 6'1" sleeping on a vinyl love seat? You may say, "He's supposed to do that. He's your husband." If you thought that, you missed it. I know a lot of men who have not been able to handle seeing their wives suffering whether through cancer treatments, mastectomies, amputations or whatever the case may be. Many men have left because they were not equipped with the tools to support and be present. Ken was there and he is still here. He has been my biggest supporter and strength, not just through this experience but through life.

To every sister who may be reading this book, if you have a man who has been there, shout him out. Celebrate him because a good man is hard to find. I am not suggesting that my husband is perfect; he's not and neither am I. However, we are perfect for each other. The only night he did not stay with me was my last night because I insisted that he go home. His strength was my strength. You never know what you have until your marriage is tested and still standing. What this generation seems to miss is that our grandparents who have been married for 50 years, are not still married because they did not have trials. They stayed together because they were committed.

As we travel the country we often let seasoned couples share and so often their testimony has been, "I am glad we stayed together." The bumps in the road like my sickness are most times only for a moment. Find something to celebrate your man for because if you don't, somebody else will. Believe me, I am the only cheerleader on his squad! I don't need anyone to join me in celebrating him. You'll catch that in the morning!

But as much as my husband was there, there was someone else who was there. He was with Daniel in the lion's den. He was with the three Hebrew boys in the fiery furnace. He was there with Joseph in the pit and prison, and He is there with you. Jesus was there and will always be there. He said, "I will never leave you nor forsake you" (Hebrews 13:5-6). This is my testimony of God's grace and mercy. When you go through your Job experience take comfort in knowing that the omnipresent God is right there with you.

My Job Experience

THE FOLLOWING PICTURES ARE
VERY GRAPHIC

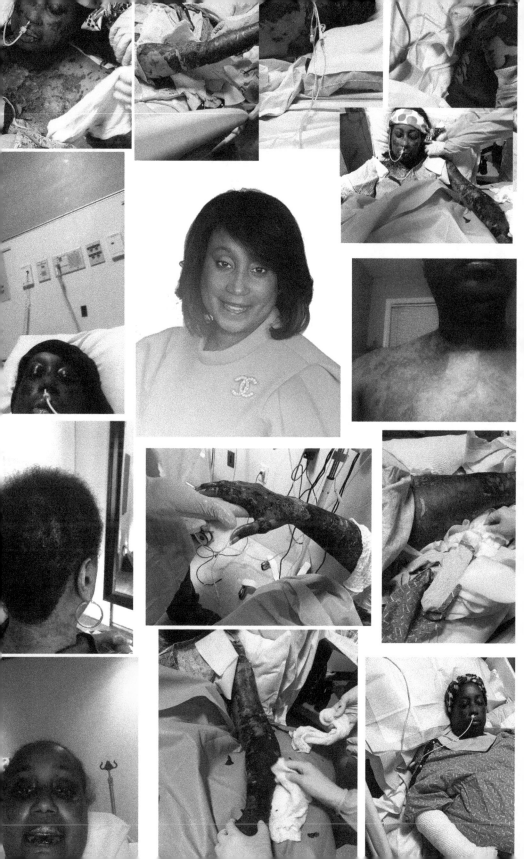

CPSIA information can be obtained
at www.ICGtesting.com
Printed in the USA
BVHW060423051020
590078BV00002B/19